Demystifying Depression

for Christians

Medical Insights for Hope and Healing

D0943159

By Dr. Gregory M. Knopf, M.D.

Published by:
In The Light Communications
Troutdale, Oregon
© 2009, 2011

Demystifying Depression *for Christians*
Medical Insights for Hope and Healing

Demystifying Depression for Christians
Medical Insights for Hope and Healing

Gregory Knopf, M.D.
p. cm.
Includes bibliographical references.
ISBN 13 - 978-0-9842177-2-4
ISBN 10 - 0-9842177-2-X (trade paper)
1. Depression, Mental—Religious aspects—Christianity.
2. Depressed persons—Religious life. I. Knopf, Gregory. II. Title.
BV4910.34.L68 2009   248.8'625—dc22 2008032486

Demystifying Depression

Table of Contents

Feeling sad, anxious, hopeless, or depressed is mystifying because there seems to be so many confusing explanations for what is causing a person to feel so bad. Instant "cures" are promised by a host of supposed experts touting everything from vitamins and herbs to positive thinking. It is no wonder that people are bewildered. Let's be perfectly honest, there is not one simple explanation for every hurting person, but the good news is there are reliable medical insights that can provide hope for genuine healing and restoration.

Major depressive disorder is a disabling, frequently recurring, but fortunately treatable medical disorder. It is the leading cause of disability among those aged 15-44 years, and is associated with an estimated 90% of suicides in the US. Patients with depression are more likely to develop stroke, diabetes, and osteoporosis. That is why depression must be aggressively evaluated and treated; people's very lives are at stake.

But how is a "depressive disorder" different from normal mood swings?

One of the hardest questions to answer is "When should medical treatment be considered?" When has the line been crossed from human emotion to medical disorder? The key to understanding is in the length and severity of the symptoms. Dr. Stephen Stahl, M.D., one of the world's leading authorities on the functions of brain chemistry, has said:

Depression is an emotion that is universally experienced by virtually everyone at some time in life. Distinguishing the "normal" emotion of depression from an illness requiring medical treatment is often problematic for those who are not trained in the mental health sciences. Stigma and misinformation in our culture create the widespread, popular misconception that . . . depression is . . . a deficiency of character, which can be overcome with effort. For example, a survey in the early 1990s of the general population revealed that 71% thought that mental illness was due to emotional weakness; 65% thought it was caused by bad parenting; 45% thought it was the victim's fault and could be willed away; 43% thought that mental illness was incurable; 35% thought it was the consequence of sinful behavior; and only 10% thought it had a biological basis or involved the brain.[1]

Dr. Stahl's point that negative stereotypes of depression abound in our culture is well taken. Contrary to the false dichotomies that exist in the public mind, there is abundant evidence of a complex mind-body interaction. This interaction, interestingly enough, makes it challenging to sort out the origins of change even at the physiological level. We know, for example, that emotional and behavioral changes made in psychotherapy—changes that involve making different choices in life—can prompt changes in brain chemistry just as much as changes in brain chemistry can prompt corresponding changes in emotions and behavior. In other words, psychological causes and brain chemistry are intricately linked to one another.

Let's say I suddenly started having some chest pain. Like most people, if I were to call my doctor's office I may get a message like this "If this is a life-threatening emergency, please hang up and dial 911 or go straight to the emergency room." How do I know if my chest pain is "life-threatening?"

We are frequently confronted by unexpected events that affect our bodies in some way; some more urgent than others, but all potentially harmful. Chest pain can be an emergency but a dark mole on your skin that is changing may not be so sudden or dramatic, and may be equally as dangerous to your health.

Without pain or other sensory indicators, we would be left helpless against serious health threats. As an alarm system, chest pain is telling us something is wrong. Not all chest pain is life-threatening "angina" from restricted blood flow to the heart muscle itself but it could be caused by a lung problem like pneumonia, a stomach problem like heartburn, or a chest wall problem like a rib fracture.

Therefore chest pain is not **the** problem; it is a signal that you **have** a problem in 1 of 4 systems in your chest.

As my great friend and co-author Dr. Gary Lovejoy has said:

> *"Depression is to the psychological self as pain is to the physical self."*

It is the alarm system that tells us we have a problem in our emotional, psychological, or physical self that needs accurate diagnosis and treatment.

The good news is that more than 90% of people can fully recover and return to normal if they receive optimal therapy. Multiple studies have shown that medication and psychotherapy are effective, but using both treatment options is better than either one alone.

By answering the following questions about depression, you will gain a better understanding of it.

1. **What is depression?**
2. **What causes depression?**
3. **How do you know if you have depression?**
4. **What are the options for effective treatment?**

1. WHAT IS DEPRESSION?

Proverbs 18:14 says *"A person's spirit sustained him in sickness, and a crushed spirit who can bear?"*

Depression is more than a temporary sad feeling; it's deeper than a bad day. People who suffer from depression are not just always disappointed. They are suffering from a debilitating emotional state that prohibits them, for one reason or another, from living their life. They push themselves through each day hoping that tomorrow will bring some kind of relief. A concise medical definition of depression is as follows:

"Depression is a syndrome characterized by a cluster of symptoms including decreased mood, problems with fatigue and motivation, physical complaints, and thoughts of suicide."

Describing depression as a **syndrome** means that the various **symptoms** that people experience as a result of this illness can be different for each individual. Even though there are many that are commonly shared, not everyone has the exact same ones or to the same degree of severity.

Depression is really an illness experienced as part of a spectrum of not only low or depressed moods but possible elevated or "manic" moods. The majority of depression is considered "unipolar" which means people only experience periods of depressed

8

mood. With more careful analysis, more people are recognizing that they can experience times of being very "up" even to the point of irrational euphoria and significant impulsivity. The treatment for people who have "up" episodes in addition to their depression is different than people who only have depressed or "down" episodes.

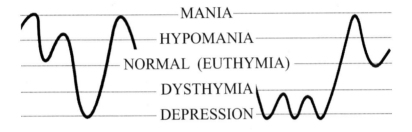

MANIA

HYPOMANIA

NORMAL (EUTHYMIA)

DYSTHYMIA

DEPRESSION

The above mood chart is a graphic representation of the spectrum that a person can experience in regards to overall mood. The center line represents normal mood or what Physicians call "euthymia." Halfway between normal mood and major depressive disorder represented by the bottom line is "dysthymia." Halfway between normal mood and mania represented by the top line is "hypomania". Mania is an abnormal state of mood where the euphoria creates significant problems including impulsivity, agitation, irritability, racing thoughts, lack of sleep, and reckless spending. "Hypomania" is simply a less extreme form of mania. A normal person may have moods that may fluctuate slightly higher or lower from the normal mood line but do not reach either hypomania or dysthymia.

Differentiating between people who only have a depressed mood versus people who can fluctuate from either a depressed mood to a euphoric mood is very important before starting the treatment process. People who only become depressed having unipolar depression, also called major depressive disorder(MDD), are treated with antidepressants to lift the mood from being depressed to normal. People who have various forms of "bipolar depression" predominantly experience significant depression but need to be treated with a "mood stabilizer" to keep them from becoming euphoric before adding an antidepressant medication to keep them from becoming depressed again during the next mood swing.

For help in determining what type of depression or other similar conditions that need to be clarified in making an accurate diagnosis, please see page 24 and Appendix A.

2. WHAT CAUSES DEPRESSION?

Understanding how the brain actually works at the cellular level can be helpful. This is a simplified explanation to provide a context as we later discuss some of the specific medical issues that cause depression. No matter what causes or triggers an episode of depression, the bottom line is that there has been a lowered level, a **depletion**, of brain hormones.

Neurotransmitter Receptor Hypothesis

Neurotransmitters are hormones or chemicals that "hand off" or "transmit" the signal from one nerve to another across a gap called the "synapse." There are many neurotransmitters, some of which have not yet been fully identified. They include: Serotonin, Norepinephrine, Acetylcholine and Dopamine.

In order to function normally, you need to have a full reservoir or "tank" of these hormones in the nerve cell ready to be released and "brigde the gap" (synapse), thus communicating the "message" to the next nerve. The concentration of these hormones must be sufficient enough to stimulate or "heat up" the "receptors" at the next nerve to create a chain reaction and "transmit" the message to the next nerve. A simplistic example of this concept would be your morning shower. Most of us will wait to step into the shower until the cold water has been flushed from the pipes by the hot water thus providing a warm shower.

If there is depletion of the neurotransmitter hormones so that the brain doesn't have an adequate amount in the reservoir, it will begin to malfunction. Depression becomes nearly synonymous with this depletion. The brain has run out of hot water. Some people have inherited a tendency to have low hormone levels because their nerve cells either break down more of the hormones than other people's do, or they do not make enough, which leaves them with a deficit situation. In either of these processes going on in the brain, these levels can be depleted either through increased demand and overuse or from inadequate production or replacement.

Figure 1. Neurotransmitters at the Synapse[2]

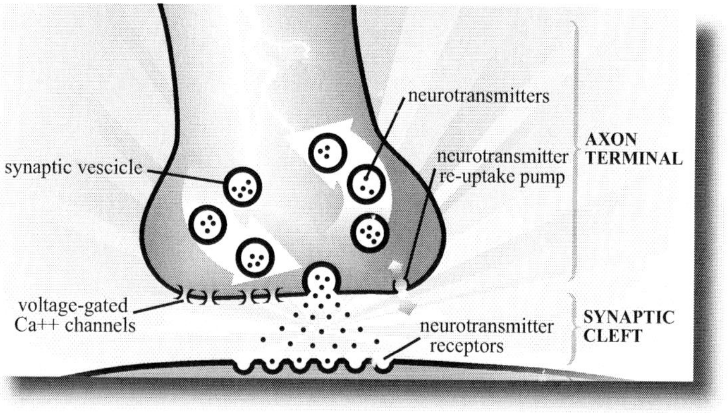

neurotransmitters

synaptic vescicle

neurotransmitter rc-uptake pump

AXON TERMINAL

voltage-gated Ca++ channels

neurotransmitter receptors

SYNAPTIC CLEFT

The brain "fills up" the tanks of serotonin, norepinephrine and dopamine during sleep. Consequently, if you do not get adequate sleep, you will be starting the next day without a normal reservoir of neurotransmitters, putting you at risk for sub-optimal functioning.

When people experience significant loss, such as a divorce or death of a child, or experience physical or emotional burnout or a number of other factors that create severe stress, the brain works overtime in anticipation of how to survive the worst possible situation. In this "full combat alert state," the mind plays a "what-if" game, expending energy trying to anticipate the worst possible scenario and make early preparation for all of the likely or unlikely possibilities. Medication can be effective in raising the level of neurotransmitter hormones to a normal level by blocking their reuptake back up into the sending nerve, which will metabolize and breakdown a significant share of these hormones. This allows the levels of hormones to be sufficient enough at the synapse so the "message" can be sent from one nerve to the next in a more normal fashion (like having instant hot water). Antidepressant medications are not addicting like Valium, narcotics or cocaine that act by directly stimulating various nerves at the synapse in certain areas of the brain and provide an altered state of consciousness or euphoria. The monoamine hypothesis of depression says that: Depression is caused by a deficiency of serotonin (5 HT) norepinephrine (NE) and/or dopamine (DA). Every known antidepressant has been shown to increase serotonin, norepinephrine, or dopamine neurotransmission.

Figure 1. Neurotransmitters at the Synapse

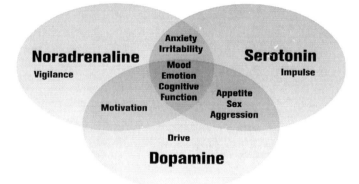

The above graph represents the association of the 3 major neurotransmitters with various mood states and symptoms associated with each of the neurotransmitters according to 2 psychopharmacologists.

For an animated visual demonstration of the synapse and how anti-depressants work, visit www.depressionoutreach.com

When is depression severe enough to consider medication?

Physicians rely on the specific DSM IV (4th edition of the Diagnostic and Statistical Manual of Mental Disorders) criteria in evaluating the following symptoms to make the diagnosis of major depressive disorder. (MDD) If a person has at least 4 of the following symptoms nearly every day for at least two weeks, you meet the criteria for depression. (1) depressed mood and feeling of hopelessness; (2)

loss of interest in daily activities and pleasures; (3) inappropriate guilt and feelings of worthlessness; (4) appetite changes causing either weight gain or weight loss; (5) sleep problems, especially early morning awakening; (6) agitation and restlessness; (7) concentration difficulties and inability to make decisions; (8) fatigue and lack of energy; (9) recurring thoughts of suicide, in which life seems empty and not worth living; 10) irritability and feeling "stressed out."

There are assessment tools (e.g., questionnaires, personality inventories, various other paper and pencil tests, and clinical interviews) that increase our accuracy in confirming the diagnosis of depression. (See appendix A for an example of various self assessment scales that can be very helpful in confirming the diagnosis of depression and monitoring response to treatment.) These scales include the Hamilton Survey for Physical and Emotional Wellness, Beck, Zung, and PHQ 9. I encourage you to consider using one or all these scales.

What is the prevalence of depression and who is at risk?

Prevalence of depression:
An estimated 11-19 million people suffer with depression at any one time.

Who is at risk?

Depression does not discriminate! It affects all ages, races, male, female, economic classes, religious/non-religious

	Lifetime	12-Month
All psychiatric disorders	48%	29.5%
Any affect is (mood) disorder	19.3%	11.3%
Any anxiety disorder	24.9%	17.2%
Any substance abuse/ dependence	26.6%	11.3%

Are there any special "at risk" times or events?

Following a significant or a perceived loss-an actual loss or a loss of a dream. During the natural transitions of adult life-puberty, midlife, menopause, PMS. Following extreme highs-"buyer's remorse" postpartum blues. Unresolved guilt-true guilt resulting from something you have done. When you've been wounded-the more important the person, the greater the hurt.

The symptoms of depression should serve as an alarm system to begin an investigation of the following areas which can cause depression:

Doctors divide the causes of depression into 2 groups, **endogenous** factors and **exogenous** factors. These terms really mean:

Endogenous- Your intrinsic or genetic potential and tendency to experience depression because of your DNA inherited from your parents. This can also include medical causes including disorders of metabolism like hypothyroidism and certain medications like interferon or reserpine. These are things that are the result of things that are **inside** you, over which you may not have a lot of control.

Exogenous- Your extrinsic or environmental factors like thinking patterns, addictions, emotional trauma, past abuse, or relational conflicts. These are things that are the result of things that have happened **to** you.

For ease of understanding, from now on we will use the following two terms:

    A. Genetic and medical factors
    B. Environmental and emotional factors

Both of these factors can adversely affect the brain and how it functions at the molecular or hormonal level causing a deficiency of specific chemicals.

The following graph may be helpful in understanding that we all have the potential to experience major depressive disorder. If you have more inherited risk factors in your family tree, you will need less environmental stress to precipitate an episode of depression than those people who do not have a similar genetic makeup.

Threshold for Depression - Ham D Scale 20

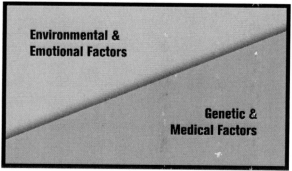

No matter where you are on this spectrum, nearly everyone can benefit from both counseling, especially for people on the left side of the graph, and medication, especially for those on the right side of the graph.

Just like the color of your eyes and hair, their is individual variability in your body's ability to manufacture or metabolize (break down) the brain hormones. It is this individuality variability that causes confusion as to why some people struggle with adversity more than others. Each person is unique thus it is important to assess on an indivdual basis the potential for significant depressions.

Some people can go through divorce, lose their job and seem to manage just fine, while others seem to collapse into depression if they get disappointed by not getting a new car. If you inherited a tendency to have low levels of these hormones, you will be more vulnerable to experiencing a chain of events that leads to depletion. In this case medication will likely be necessary to provide relief.

Can significant depletion be caused by long-term emotional stress? Yes. Can significant depletion be caused by an environmental stressor? Yes. Can significant depletion be caused by family genetics? Yes. Therefore, how should the issue of using medications be viewed? As a necessary evil? As something to avoid at all costs? Is medication a panacea that should be given to everyone?

The good news is that 90 percent of people can be helped significantly with their depression once they have found a suitable medication. And with this help, they are much more amenable to the work of psychotherapy, which can bring about lasting change, and the possibility of tapering off medication.

A. Role of genetics and medical factors

With the decoding of the human genome, some researchers thought we might be able to discover "the depression gene." Most experts believe this is highly unlikely. Even though there is not "one gene" for diabetes, people inherit multiple genes and therefore are predisposed to develop diabetes if they become significantly overweight or eat too much sugar. Some experts believe that there may be say 100 genes that can "predispose" or increase the likelihood that a person can develop medical depression. If in individual has any 20 of the potential 100 "depression genes," they are at increased risk of becoming depressed with or without a "trigger" or inciting stressful event that occurs in their life. This explains why there is so much variability in the kind and severity of symptoms that people can experience, and why there is so much difference in how a person responds to various medications. A specific antidepressant that works great for one person may cause incapacitating side effects for another person.

Risk factors related to genetics:
Family history-very critical because we inherit the potential to have depression from our parents.

Prior personal history-people can experience depression and come out of it for a significant period of time.

Female gender- Approximately 70% are women, and 30% are men. May actually be closer to 60% women and 40% men because men often deny or minimize their symptoms.

Other psychiatric disorders-like general anxiety disorder which may precede depression or "co-exist" with depression so that a person has both.

Substance abuse-Ecstasy destroys serotonin cells. We only have 250,000 total serotonin cells in the brain and each cell has "connections" with 500,000 other cells. The serotonin cells that are destroyed will not re-generate. This will leave your brain permanently deficient in the essential neurotransmitter serotonin.

Other substances of abuse like cocaine and methamphetamine will destroy dopamine cells in a similar fashion.

Alcohol-Many people, especially men, will use alcohol to "treat" their depression because they are in denial. Sometimes antidepressant medications can help people recover from alcohol addiction if they do have underlying depression.

Prescription medications-Many medications will increase a person's risk of developing depression. Approximately 80% of people who are treated with interferon will experience depression and need to be treated with antidepressants. For a list of other medications please see appendix D.

Medical conditions-
Cancer-any kind of cancer especially pancreas, breast, prostate, leukemia, lymphoma. See appendix E.

Brain trauma or disease-postconcussion syndrome, stroke, multiple sclerosis, Parkinson's disease, dementia and Alzheimers.

Cardiovascular diseases-coronary artery disease increases your risk between 18 and 20%.
Endocrine disorders-diabetes and hypothyroidism. See appendix E.

Chronic pain syndromes and fibromyalgia. Dr. Allen Bott M.D., neurologist and psychiatrist from Oakland California has said that he believes that fibromyalgia is "actually depression without the mood component." It is significant that two of the three

FDA approved medications to treat fibromyalgia, (Cymbalta and Savella) are thought to work by restoring the proper balance of norepinephrine and serotonin in the spinal cord fluid.

Menopause and perimenopause. -Several years ago, a woman came to me as a result of hearing that I was skillful in prescribing medications for depression. She had been experiencing extreme sadness, crying all the time and feeling hopeless. She had never felt this way before in her life. Her husband was in the military and she had an ovarian tumor that resulted in a complete hysterectomy and removal of both ovaries. Ever since that surgery, she had experienced a profound mood change. Her doctor had given her an estrogen patch to use for hormone replacement. She said, "I guess I need to be put on medication." Fortunately, I did not provide a prescription assuming she simply needed anti-depressants even though her Hamilton Survey indicated she was depressed. I suggested that her depression could be caused by a lack of estrogen that was not being absorbed adequately through her skin. If that was the case she might not need anti-depressants. We checked an estrogen blood level which came back low, so I switched her to oral estrogen pills and her depression resolved! Therefore, many women, but not all, are extremely sensitive to the lack of estrogen in their body and they will experience true depression which should be treated with female hormones and not anti-depressants.

B. Environmental and emotional factors:

Risk factors:
Life stressors-Death of a spouse, child, loss of job, financial problems, or relational conflict.

Certain personality traits-like being perfectionistic; you can never feel good or satisfied about anything you do because you fail to measure up to an impossible standard. This is very common within the Christian community. Another trait is being a "people pleaser" where you feel that you are always the victim of circumstances or are at the mercy of others.

Loss of parents at an early age or childhood abuse-emotional trauma or abandonment at an early age can cause certain neurons to be "pruned" during development that can help a child to "survive" and adapt which later in life becomes maladaptive and increases the risk of developing depression.

True guilt from unresolved conflict or from unconfessed sin-Example is King David when he sinned with Bathsheba. **Psalm 32,51.**

Inaccurate concept of God-If a person sees God as a harsh task master who can never be appeased or pleased. Therefore you can not experience a healthy relationship with God. (See Light on the Fringe: Finding Hope in the Darkness of Depression for an extensive explanation of healthy and unhealthy concepts of God.)

3. HOW DO YOU KNOW IF YOU HAVE DEPRESSION?

One of the difficulties in diagnosing and treating depression is that some of the common symptoms that accompany depression can also be seen in other conditions. I explain the following diagram to my patients:

Overlapping Symptoms

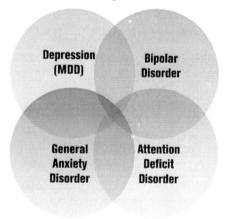

The 4 interlocking circles represent major depressive disorder, bipolar spectrum disorders (there are many subtypes of bipolar disorder), general anxiety disorder and anxiety subtypes like PTSD (posttraumatic stress disorder), seasonal affective disorder, social anxiety disorder, and panic disorders etc. The last circle is attention deficit disorder either with inattention or hyperactivity and anxiety. People with attention deficit disorder often feel anxious that they will forget something; therefore their mind is always on "hyper alert" so they cannot focus or finish the task that is at hand. People can have "co-morbid" conditions which mean they have an overlap of more than one process going on at the same time. Another synonym is "dual diagnosis." Many people have both bipolar 2 and attention deficit disorder and they will benefit from treating both conditions simultaneously.

Therefore, a person should honestly review the preceding list of symptoms and potential risk factors based of their family inheritance, medical conditions, medications, history of substance abuse, and environmental trauma. The "Hamilton Survey for Physical and Emotional Wellness"would be a helpful questionaire for you to take. If your 25 question total score is 7 or less, it is very unlikely that you have depression. If your score is between 8 and 19 you may be experiencing dysthymia and should consider some type of nonmedication options discussed in this book and monitor your symptoms. If your score is 20 or greater, you have a high likelihood that you could be experiencing (medical) major depressive disorder (MDD) and should discuss treatment options with your doctor including medications and counseling or psychotherapy. For completeness, I would suggest taking the Hirschfeld Mood Disorders Questionnaire which can suggest bipolar disorder, the ARDS questionnaire which can indicate attention deficit disorder, and the GAD-7 which can confirm General Anxiety Disorder. (see appendix A) You can obtain a printable version of these 4 scales at www.depressionoutreach.com.

What does an episode of depression look like?

The course of treated depression follows some clearly definable stages. The following is a graphic representation of a depressive episode with the various possible outcomes.

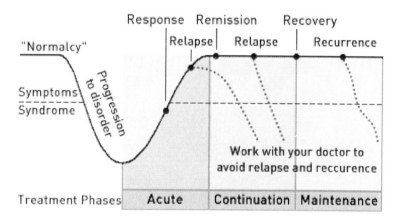

Kupfer Curve: developed by Dr David Kupfer M.D.

Schematic of the Neuronal Synapse- go to:

http://en.wikipedia.org/wiki/
Image:SynapseIllustration2.svg

Figure 2. Kupfer Curve[3]

The term "response" generally means that a depressed patient has experienced at least a 50 percent reduction in symptoms as assessed by the

Hamilton Depression Rating Scale. "Relapse" is the term used when a person gets worse after treatment began to work but the person had not "gotten well." "Remission" is the term used when essentially all symptoms have gone away and the person is feeling totally normal. "Recovery" means that the remission has lasted for at least 6 to 12 months. "Recurrence" means the symptoms of depression have returned, causing significant problems in functioning and mood.

Clinical Example:
One of the best things about being a family doctor is the opportunity to develop long-term relationships with a wide variety of people in the community. The fact that people would trust me to share the sacred space of the most intimate issues regarding their person and body is humbling and kept in utmost confidence.

As I glanced over the list of people I was to see one afternoon, I recognized a familiar name of someone who is a marriage and family counselor in the community. I assumed that I would be seeing him for some type of medical problem like back pain, sore neck, or bronchitis. As I entered the room, John and I exchanged a warm greeting before I opened his chart to begin the office visit. To my surprise, John began describing a long history lasting multiple years of severe mood swings. Recently they had become so bad that he was having thoughts of suicide. He expressed total frustration in the fact that in his role as counselor he had helped innumerable people in similar situations achieve relief from their sense of hopelessness. "I know all the right answers and have studied all the books and yet I find myself totally incapable of experiencing relief," John said.

His medical history revealed a man who had been in excellent physical health his entire life. He had never taken any long-term medications, had grown up in a Christian family, was successful in his career and was enjoying a strong relationship with his wife and children. It wasn't until we began discussing his mother's health that the pieces of the puzzle began to fit. John's mother had suffered a "nervous breakdown" after the birth of her fifth child and, for the rest of her life, suffered severe bouts of depression, to the point of needing hospitalization several times and receiving ECT (Electroconvulsive Therapy), a type of treatment reserved for only the most severe and resistant cases of depression.

Given his professional background, it took courage for John to acknowledge the symptoms that had been plaguing him for so long. There has been a tendency in the Christian community to embrace a set of assumptions that can be greatly damaging. There is an implicit assumption, for example, that if you live a life obedient to God, you will be shielded from emotional pain or severe hopelessness. Likewise, reminiscent of the counsel of Job's friends, there is the implied contract that you will have God's continued protection only if you are obedient in confessing every sin.

After learning of John's family history and his struggles with suicide, I had John take my Hamilton Survey for Physical and Emotional Wellness. His score revealed significant depression. Because John was having associated symptoms of agitation and fidgeting as well as irritability, I elected to try John on the "dual-acting" antidepressant Effexor XR which enhances both the serotonin and norepinephrine neurotransmitter systems. I gave him some samples to try and asked him to return in three weeks. John's experience was somewhat unusual but not rare. He described such a dramatic change in his symptoms that he said, "It was like the clouds parted and the sun began to shine on me." It was an entirely new experience for him after he started taking the medication.

This kind of response is the exception rather than the rule but does illustrate the point that some people do have an inherited tendency that can only be adequately treated with medical intervention. John's prognosis is excellent, but he will probably require a maintenance dose of medication for the rest of his life.

Even with biological depressions, the message is the same: We are exquisitely designed with emotional alarm systems to tell us when it is time to take action so that we might be restored to the fulfillment of our God-given desires. There is no greater upside to the experience of depression than to meaningfully

29

grow through our pain. In the end, is this not what Jesus meant when He spoke of living in the kingdom of God now? The abundant life He promised is not the easy life or necessarily the prosperous life as the world measures prosperity. It is the fulfilling life, the life of wisdom that understands the importance of what makes the difference for eternity.

Why is depression under diagnosed and under treated?

Approximately 20 every 100 patients visiting their primary care physician will have clinically significant depression, but only 1 of the 20 will tell the doctor about their symptoms. Such underreporting results in misdiagnosis and inadequate treatment. Of all the patients who suffer from depression, only 50% are receiving any treatment and less than half of those are getting "adequate care."

Some of the major contributing factors include: (1) stigma—it is not "okay" for some people to take antidepressant medications because it is considered "drug abuse"; (2) lack of public knowledge as to what depression is, its various subtypes and how it can be treated; (3) lack of reporting of depressed mood—only 17 percent of people who are eventually diagnosed with depression actually go to their doctor complaining about a depressed mood; Likelihood that depression is the cause if people have the following complaints:

Sleep disturbance-especially early morning awakening	61%
Fatigue: (Medical causes need to be evaluated first)	60%
Nonspecific musculoskeletal complaints: (Fibromyalgia)	43%

(4) depressive symptoms are often masked by physical symptoms like fatigue or associated medical illnesses, including low thyroid, heart attacks and sleep apnea; (5) poor medication prescribing and follow-through on the part of physicians who are not fully knowledgeable and skilled in using the newer and more effective medications. There is also pressure on doctors from insurance companies to only use "generic" (cheapest) medications because they insist that "all anti-depressants are equally effective" which in my opinion and many other doctors is **not** true. As a result, some people will not be able to achieve full remission of their symptoms because they are on the wrong medication.

What are some of the reasons that people avoid considering medication?

Underestimation of the seriousness of the symptoms.

Stigma or feeling ashamed that the diagnosis is correct.

Side effects of the medication (like sexual side effects.) Fear of dependency or "addiction."

Concern of interfering with the success of psychotherapy or counseling.

Depression is temporary so as soon as you are feeling better you can stop taking the medication.

Many patients with depression believe they are not worthy of feeling better.

What about anxiety and depression? How are they related?

Anxiety disorders, particularly generalized anxiety disorder (GAD) frequently occur along with depression, one third the time starting before, one third of the time starting after, and one third of the time starting at the same time as the depression.

Patients with anxious depression are significantly less likely and often take longer to achieve remission in patients with non-anxious depression, and in older adults with depression, severe anxiety symptoms predicted longer delays and lower rates of remission.

4. WHAT ARE THE OPTIONS FOR EFFECTIVE TREATMENT

Should non-medication treatments be tried first?
It is useful to do an assessment of a person's current lifestyle. Am I simply exhausted, and need more sleep? Am I experiencing loneliness through death or loss of a relationship? Am I angry or bitter over an injustice? Am I physically depleted and in need of proper nutrition and exercise? (Regular exercise improves brain hormone levels.) Have I taken steps to nurture my spiritual life?

You may want to immerse your mind with scripture and meditate on significant passages. You may want to listen to uplifting music. (King Saul probably suffered from depression, maybe even bipolar disorder, and the music from young David's harp was therapeutic for him. Remember he ultimately committed suicide) If a person has done all these things and is still experiencing significant problems in mood, I believe it is time to see their doctor.

If these or other alternative treatments do not provide significant relief of the depressive symptoms within 1-2 months, or cause side effects, it would be unwise to delay in seeing your physician any longer.

What about St. John's Wort, SAMe and other alternatives to prescription medication?

St. John's Wort is an herb that does have an affect on the brain hormones although its effect is considered to be milder than prescription medications. Simply because it is nonprescription does not mean it is safe. Many people can experience elevations of blood pressure if they eat certain foods like cheese, beans or wine. St. John's Wort should not be taken with other prescription medications, and there may be some evidence of early cataract formation with exposure to sunlight. In my experience, taking St. John's Wort has not been all that helpful for most people and does pose some risks to a person's health.

There are studies that suggest taking SAMe or adding it to antidepressant medication can be helpful, particularly for patients who prefer supplements.

"If these or other alternative treatments do not provide significant relief of the depressive symptoms within 1-2 months, or cause side effects, it would be unwise to delay in seeing your physician any longer."

What about Vitamin D and depression?

A number of medical studies report some connection between vitamin D levels and the risk of depression. Low vitamin D levels may be related to depression rather than contributing to the disorder.

Vitamin D may lower the risk of depression by:

- Reducing the risk of diseases that may trigger depression, such as cancer, cardiovascular disease, and multiple sclerosis.

- Reducing the production of cytokines. Cytokines are proteins that increase inflammation and have been shown to be a possible risk factor for depression.

There are currently no reported studies showing that vitamin D supplements reduce the risk of depression. However, given the evidence, it is possible that vitamin D could have a positive effect on those who suffer from depression, and at least will not do harm.

There is increasing evidence that vitamin D affects all parts of the body, including the brain. Thus, it is reasonable to think that having higher vitamin D levels would reduce the risk of depressive disorder.

Are depression and weight problems connected?

Since eating food actually raises brain serotonin levels, depression can result in overeating behavior. Therefore, some people are "treating" their depression by overeating without knowing it. Some of my patients who have a "food addiction" lost a substantial amount of weight when I prescribed buproprion (Wellbutrin) because it reduced their food cravings.

What if I choose not to use medication and just "tough it out?"

Non-treatment can have serious consequences-dementia (Alzheimer's) and suicide

Consequences of nontreatment or inadequate treatment of depression:
There is some evidence that over extended periods of time if people remain depressed as a result of low brain serotonin and norepinephrine levels, actual shrinkage in the hippocampus(deep part of the brain) can occur which could potentially be associated with increased likelihood of Alzheimer's type dementia. There is evidence that when neurotransmitter levels are depleted, this causes low levels of BDNF, (brain derived neurotrophic factor) which causes brain neurons to shrink and eventually die. Raising levels of serotonin and norepinephrine with the use of antidepressants also increases the brains level of BDNF, and encourages the "regrowth" of neurons.

More than 60% of people who committed suicide have been depressed with a major depressive disorder. About 8% of people with major depressive disorder will die by suicide.

Risk factors for suicide:

Diagnosis of a chronic depressive disorder
Past history of suicide attempts or suicidal thoughts

Family history of suicide
Depressive episodes requiring hospitalization
Change from inpatient to outpatient status
Severe worrisome anxiety symptoms
Panic attacks (recent history)
Severe loss of pleasure in life
Alcohol abuse: moderate or worse

What about counseling? Does it work?

Multiple studies have proven that counseling and psychotherapy plus medication are more effective than either one alone. For many people, counseling and psychotherapy alone can lead to healing and resolution of depression. But just like getting on the "right" medication, finding a skillful counselor who can help you resolve emotional, relational, and spiritual issues may take time. You may want to check out the web site for the American Association of Christian Counselors, aacc.net to find a Christian counselor in your area. I would get a list of potential counselors and then ask your pastor, physician and friends for a recommendation. Pray that God will provide guidance in finding the counselor who is best suited for you.

Don't anti-depressants increase your risk of suicide?

In 2004, the FDA issued a "black box" warning to physicians that anti-depressant may cause increased suicidal **thinking** in young people under 19 years of age. As a result, physicians became more cautious about prescribing anti-depressants, and many people became afraid to start taking them. In 2008, the *American Journal of Psychiatry* published an article that showed that as a result of the FDA warning, deaths from suicides actually increased 14%. Thomas Insel of the National Institute of Mental Health said, "We may have inadvertently created a problem by putting a "black box" warning on medications that were useful. If the drugs were doing more harm than good, then the reduction in prescription rates should mean the risk of suicide should go way down, and it hasn't gone down at all-it has gone up." He concludes by saying, "If I had a child with depression, I would go after the best treatment but also provide close monitoring."

What medication should I take?

Just like trying on a pair of shoes, there is no one medication that is perfect for everyone. Not only are there differences in a person's susceptibility to depression, but there is also individual variability in a person's response to medications. This makes the prescribing of antidepressants closer to "trial and error" than "one size fits all." In many people, Prozac will initially stimulate and energize those who are depressed or sluggish, but later on they will be sedated. Sometimes the medication begins to lose its effectiveness after a person has been on the pills for a period of time. Some psychiatrists call this the "poop-out" effect. If the medication causes significant side effects, it should be stopped and a different medication tried. Most likely, one of the medications available today will significantly help you feel good without creating significant side effects.

If a person is having mood problems as well as problems with memory, ability to concentrate, maintaining attention and experiencing fatigue, they should be considered for a medication that would boost their levels of the norepinephrine neurotransmitter. If they are having mood problems associated with anxiety, panic disorder or phobias of multiple types, including social phobias as well as obsessive-compulsive problems, they should be considered for medication that would primarily increase the levels of serotonin.

The best analogy that I have ever heard to explain the difference between serotonin and norepinephrine was given at a lecture by nationally recognized psychiatrist Dr Michael A. Schwartz M.D. He said that being deficient in serotonin is like driving in the mountains in the dark of night and in the road ahead is a deer that is "frozen" by the intensity of the headlights. The deer is essentially "paralyzed" by fear and can not figure out which way to run to avoid being hit by the car. People who are low on serotonin have no "dimmer switch." They are anxious, tense, nervous and tend to obsess over trivial things. These people usually respond to SSRI's. (Selective Serotonin Reuptake Inhibitors) In contrast, being deficient in norepinephrine is like driving your car in such a dense fog that you have to slow down to 5 miles per hour because you can not see 10 feet in front of you. People who are deficient in norepinephrine feel tired and exhausted, have difficulty concentrating, and can not get motivated. These people respond to medications that raise the levels of norepinephrine in their brain. This explains why those who are tired are given SSRI's, often feel "blah" and those who are anxious but are given medication to increase norepinephrine will feel more tense, agitated, and anxious. Therefore, by tailoring the medication to restore which ever neurotransmitter (or both) that is deficient; you can bring that person back into remission (back to normal) in the shortest possible time.

Some of the latest scientific evidence indicates that using medications that increase *both* serotonin and norepinephrine levels may be superior in helping a person recover from depression as compared to medications that work on either serotonin or norepinephrine alone, because many people have symptoms that indicate they are deficient in both neurotransmitters. Medications like Effexor XR, Cymbalta, and Pristiq raise the levels of both serotonin and norepinephrine. Many times physicians will use combinations of antidepressants to obtain full remission and lower the amount of side affects. In essence, using more than one medication can provide greater effectiveness while reducing the overall number of side effects.

With major depressive disorder, the following picture explains how the different antidepressants help restore the depleted brain neurotransmitters. Think of a tank that holds the 3 major neurotransmitters, serotonin, norepinephrine, and dopamine. If you are deficient from either using up too much or do not make enough, there are only 2 options:

1. Conserve what you have already made, or
2. Increase production of more neurotransmitter.

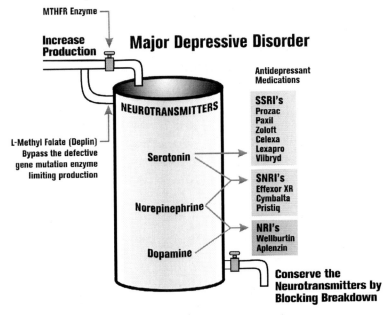

1. Conservation: If a person was low in serotonin, they could improve their mood and decrease their anxiety by blocking the breakdown of serotonin by using either Prozac, Paxil, Zoloft, Celexa, Lexapro, or Viibryd. If a person was

low in both serotonin and norepinephrine in order to improve their mood, anxiety, and fatigue they could first try either Effexor, Cymbalta, or Pristiq. If a person was low on norepinephrine and dopamine, in order to improve their mood and decrease their fatigue they could first try Wellbutrin.

2. Increase Production: Many people have a genetic mutation of MTHFR (methyl tetrahydrofolate reductase) enzyme which prevents a person from making enough serotonin, norepinephrine, and dopamine. There is a blood test that can detect this genetic defect.

In 2008 a new class of medications called "tri-monoamine modulators," represented by Deplin, (L.-methyl folate), was approved to enhance effectiveness of all antidepressant medications. You can either prove you have a problem by getting the blood test done or simply try Deplin to see if it helps. It works by bypassing the blockage to normal production caused by the genetic mutation and allow your body to have enough "building blocks" to make more of the neurotransmitters. Up to 30% of people who have not achieved "remission" can be significantly helped by adding Deplin, which is a prescription pill even though it is actually considered a "medical food" by the FDA.

(See Appendix C for a list of the major medications currently available with my assessment of the advantages, disadvantages and personal recommendations as to the situations in which they are most likely to work best. See also Appendix D for treatment guidelines regarding medication priorities that increase the chance for a successful outcome on the first try rather than a more random choice process).

What if I don't get better with the medication?

"Treatment resistant depression" is defined as a failure to respond to at least 2 different antidepressants at the appropriate dose and length of treatment.

Medication options to achieve relief from of all symptoms (full remission) usually involve either:

1. "switching" to a medication in a different class
2. "add-on" therapy (augmentation) with a second antidepressant that is complimentary or a medication other than an antidepressant to enhance the partial improvement already achieved

Using patient self assessment tools to monitor progress is essential to identifying the residual symptoms that can otherwise appear patient function and increase relapse risk. A patient's absence of response to 1 therapeutic agent suggests the need to switch to another, possibly one from a different class, whereas a partial response provides a strong rationale for augmentation or combination therapy.

How long should a person take medication?

Rule of thirds: Approximately one-third of people will experience a single episode of significant depression usually precipitated by a major traumatic event. Treatment is usually required for at least six months and then the medication can be phased out. This is somewhat similar to a physician using a cast to hold the broken bone of the leg in proper alignment so the bone can develop a strong union. Counseling and psychotherapy can often promote healing and resolution of depressive symptoms and lessen the likelihood of relapse. Approximately one-third of people will experience relapses of depression. If you have had more than one episode of depression requiring medication, your chances are greater than 80 percent that you will require medication at some time in the future to treat another episode. Approximately one-third of people have a more prolonged type of depression, usually inherited, which is best treated with long-term medication.

CONCLUSIONS:

The symptoms of depression, feeling hopeless, helpless, and worthless, are very common. See it like an alarm system to guide you to investigate the possible causes. Take steps to evaluate the issues whether they are genetic (inside) or environmental (outside) and seek proper medical and psychological help. It is not because you are "emotionally weak."

Depression will affect you in every way: Your body, your mind, your emotions, and your spirit. Therefore, assessment and treatment must address each of those areas.

Depression is evidence that brain hormones (neurotransmitters) are depleted. Most people are more aware and open about the physical symptoms of the depression than the psychological symptoms of their depression. There can be multiple triggers or inciting events, so do not be afraid to talk with your doctor or counselor and ask for help and advice. Most people are more aware and open about the physical symptoms of the depression than the psychological symptoms of their depression.

There is no blood test to make a diagnosis of depression, but a careful professional assessment can be highly accurate.

Many Christian people feel ashamed that they need to

take antidepressant medication because they feel they have disappointed God by their choices or behavior.

Some people are afraid antidepressants are "addictive" which they are not. 95% of people with depression can be dramatically helped with appropriate antidepressant medication and counseling/psychotherapy if needed.

Be patient to find the right antidepressant that works the best for you. Remember most medications will have a few nuisance side effects, but most disappear or diminish with time.

It can be very difficult and sometimes impossible to "fix yourself" with sheer willpower.

There are so many myths and misinformation in our culture that prevents people from breaking free from the bondage and brokenness that characterizes depression. Suggesting that taking antidepressants is a sign of emotional weakness or the same as using mind altering drugs like marijuana or cocaine demonstrates a profound lack of understanding of neurophysiology.

Doing nothing can have serious consequences and increase your risk of dementia and Alzheimer's disease if depression is left untreated for years. It is so tragic to see people suffer needlessly when so much is available to fully restore them to normal functioning in all areas of life.

FINAL THOUGHTS:

How does God view those who are depressed?
I believe God is intimately involved in the healing
process of our spirit, soul, and body to experience
wholeness.

I Thessalonians 5:23 The Message
*May God himself, the God who makes everything holy and
whole, make you holy and whole, put you together — spirit,
soul, and body — and keep you fit for the coming of our
Master, Jesus Christ. The One who called you is completely
dependable. If he said it, he'll do it!*

His desire is for our good and He does not use
depression to punish us.

Jeremiah 29:11-14 NIV
*"For I know the plans I have for you," declares the Lord,
"plans to prosper you and not to harm you, plans to give
you hope and a future. Then you will call upon me, and
I will listen to you. You will seek me and find me when
you seek me with all your heart. I will be found by you,":*
declares the Lord.

And as result of His movement in our lives, He gives
us the privilege of helping others.

II Corinthians 1:5,6 The Message
*…"Jesus the Messiah! Father of all mercy! God of all
healing counsel! He comes alongside us when we go
through hard times, and before you know it, he brings*

alongside someone else who is going through hard times so that we can be there for that person just as God was there for us."

What would happen in our society if individual Christians as well as churches made a conscious effort to live out our Christian calling to "bear one another's burdens?"

What would happen if rather than avoiding those who are hurting or "in a bad place," we actually came along side them with encouragement to seek help by considering an evaluation for counseling or medical treatment, and participation in a Christian group or fellowship? What if churches actually paid for office visit fees for those in their church without insurance and are in need medical attention? There is nothing greater in life than to see others find freedom and wholeness in Christ!

Romans 6:19 The Message
"How much different it is now as you live in God's freedom, your lives healed and expansive in holiness." God could choose to heal someone instantaneously, but I believe He more often uses available medical therapies as well as effective counseling and psychotherapy to accomplish full restoration. God truly is the "Great Physician!"

My final prayer for all of us is captured in this statement from **Romans 15:13 NIV:**
"May the God of hope fill you with all joy and peace as you trust in him, so that you may overflow with hope by the power of the Holy Spirit."

APPENDIX A

Hamilton Survey For
Emotional And Physical Wellness
Dr. Gregory Knopf

INSTRUCTIONS: Think over the past two weeks and rate yourself for each question as you identify with the phrases, symptoms and feelings.

Rating Scale:
0=None, 1=Mild, 2=Moderate, 3=Severe, 4=Extreme

_____1) Depressed Mood: I find myself feeling very sad and helpless, either because of the present circumstances or for no reason at all. I feel a sense of hopelessness that things will never get better. I find myself crying more frequently and am not able to "hold it together." I often feel worthless.

_____2) Guilt Feelings: I sometimes feel like I should be punished. I really do not like myself right now and maybe I deserve some of the things that are happening to me. Even though I can't think of specific examples, I feel guilty much of the time.

_____3) Suicide: I often find myself thinking about death and sometimes wish that I didn't have to live anymore. My life seems empty and not worth the effort it is taking. I find myself wanting to avoid other people and be alone. I've told at least one other person that it would be better if I were dead or gone. Sometimes I find myself wanting to cut myself or think about taking a lot of pills.

_____4) Initial Insomnia: I have difficulty falling asleep after I get into bed at night.

_____5) Middle Insomnia: I have difficulty sleeping all night long without interruption. I wake up for no reason several times During the night. I sometimes get back to sleep and sometimes not.

_____6) Delayed Insomnia: I find myself waking up 2-3 hours before I want to, for no reason, and cannot get back to sleep.

_____7) Work and interest: My job and family are no longer enjoyable. I often find myself not caring about my job or home responsibilities. I rarely do any of the hobbies that I used to enjoy. My friends invite me to do things, but I often find reasons to say no. The things that I use to enjoy don't seem to lift my spirits. People at work are noticing that the quality of my work has deteriorated. My family members are beginning to complain that I don't do the usual things around the house that I did in the past.

_____8) Alertness: I find myself feeling sluggish in my ability to think, communicate my ideas, and sometimes just moving around.

_____9) Agitation: I find myself fidgeting and feeling very restless. Often I will pace back and forth or sometimes clench my fists. Sometimes I will tap my feet or hands for no reasons or bite my lips. I often find myself wringing my hands. Sometimes I will pull at my hair or pick at my fingernails or clothes.

_____10) Anxiety (Psychological): I often feel tense and unable to relax. I find myself irritable with family or coworkers. I am easily startled. Even though I try not to, I often worry over trivial matters. Often, I am fearful for no reason. I have a sense that things are going to get worse and I will be unable to do anything to change it. I feel out of control and that I could have a panic attack.

_____11) Anxiety (Physical): I often times have "butterflies" in my stomach. Many times my stomach will cramp or I will have indigestion. Recently I have noted more belching or diarrhea. My heart has begun to beat much faster that it used to. I often find myself feeling like I can't get enough air. Sometimes I have noted tingling in my fingers or around my mouth. I am sweating more than I used to or feel flushed. I have noticed that my hands have begun to shake slightly. I have recently started having headaches for no reason. I find that I have to go to the bathroom and urinate more frequently, and often smaller amounts.

_____12) Loss of Appetite: Food no longer seems appealing to me. I just don't feel like eating as much as I used to. My friends have expressed concern about my eating habits.

_____13) Fatigue: I feel exhausted almost all the time. I no longer have the kind of energy to function like I used to. I often feel like my arms or legs are heavy. I have wondered if I have "chronic fatigue syndrome."

_____14) Sexual: I have lost my desire for sexual intimacy that I used to have. I am finding that it is not worth the effort to be involved in sex.

_____15) Fear: I am afraid that I might have cancer or something really bad affecting my health. I think a lot about many kinds of symptoms which I have never had before, and it upsets me.

_____16) Weight Loss: I am now losing weight, even though I am not trying to lose weight.

_____17) Unexplained Pains: I have pain in my muscles and around my joints and along my spine. Doctors have not given me a clear reason for the pains because they consider the symptoms too vague. I wonder if I could have " fibromyalgia." I often have headaches and low back pains.

_____18) Mood Swings: I find that my moods can range from high to low, often for no reason, and even on the same day. It upsets me to think that I cannot control my emotions when I am down.

_____19) Oversleeping: I am finding that it is harder to get up in the morning, even though I go to bed on time. I don't get the kind of sleep I would like, and stay in bed for hours at a time.

_____20) Oversleeping: I am sleeping more than ever before. It seems that all I want to do is sleep.

_____21) Napping: It is difficult for me to get through the day without taking a nap or wanting to take a nap. I am so tired by the afternoon that when I come home I can hardly function.

_____22) Increased Appetite: I am finding myself eating more even if I am not hungry. I am having more cravings than ever for certain foods like chocolate. I am eating more during my regular meals and having snacks between meals. My friends have expressed concern about my eating habits. I sometimes binge on junk food.

_____23) Weight Gain: I have gained weight recently. It seems like I am gaining weight even though I am not eating enough to explain the increase.

_____24) Sluggishness: I oftentimes feel almost paralyzed in my ability to process my thoughts and feelings. I am unable to find the will power to do the things I need to do. I just can't think as quickly as I used to.

_____25) Physical Movement: I feel sluggish physically. People ask me if there is something wrong because they say I look sad.

_____ ITEM TOTAL

Guide to interpreting total score:

• 0-7 Normal

• 8-19 Mild "dysthymia" or "sub-clinical depression"

• 20-29 "mild to moderate" major depressive disorder (MDD)

• 30-39 "moderately severe" major depressive disorder (MDD)

• Greater than 40 is consistent with "severe" major depressive disorder (MDD)

Note: A downloadable version of the Hamilton Survey For Emotional and Physical Wellness is available at our website, DepressionOutreach.com.

More online resources:

Visit www.depressionoutreach.com for:
Bipolar Disorder Questionnaire:
>   MDQ (Mood Disorder Questionnaire) by Dr. Hirschfeld

>   Also available at www.dbsalliance.org/pdfs/ MDQ.pdf

General Anxiety Disorder Questionnaire:
>   GAD 7

Adult Attention Deficit Disorder Questionnaire:
>   ASRS (Adult Self-Rated Scale)

To access other, easy to take, alternative depression scales (such as the Zung Self Rated Depression Scale, the Beck Self Rated Scale, or the PHQ-9 Scale), which you may wish to review, you can go to each of the following internet links:

Zung Self Rated Scale:
http://healthnet.umassmed.edu/mhealth/ ZungSelfRatedDepressionScale.pdf

Beck Self Rated Scale:
http://www.ibogaine.desk.nl/graphics/3639b1c_23.pdf

PHQ-9 Depression Questionnaire:
http://www.mhqp.org/mhqp_attachments/PHQ-9%20 depression%20screening%20tool.pdf

APPENDIX B

Irrational Beliefs:
Results And Counter Beliefs

The following are the most common irrational beliefs and their rational counter beliefs as measured by the Irrational Beliefs Test (IBT). The IBT is an independently scored inventory containing a hundred statements. The test taker is asked to agree or disagree with each statement on a 5 point scale to determine the strength of their beliefs. It is useful for identifying the dysfunctional ideologies of those suffering from depression and anxiety. These irrational beliefs lead to a variety of agitated feelings and behaviors that block a more adaptive lifestyle. As you will notice, most of them support a life of self-victimization. The following is a breakdown.

IRRATIONAL BELIEF and WHAT IT LEADS TO	RATIONAL BELIEF
1 It is a dire necessity for me to be loved and approved of by virtually every person who is significant to me in any way. **RESULT:** Leads to a *desperate search for social approval* as a criterion for self-acceptance. It often reflects an underlying self-hatred.	While it is nice to be loved and approved of by certain select people, it is not necessary. My self-worth does not depend on the approval of others.
2 I should be thoroughly competent, adequate and achieving in every respect if I am to consider myself worthwhile. **RESULT:** Leads to a *paralyzing fear of failure* where performance becomes the basis for all personal worth.	Being competent and achieving in some areas certainly has its rewards, but my self-worth has nothing to do with my level of performance.
3 Certain people are bad, wicked or villainous and they should be severely blamed and punished for their villainy. **RESULT:** Leads to a lot of *blaming behavior* where fault finding and accusations are the major preoccupation.	While certain people may do bad, wicked or villainous things, they still have personal worth. Negative consequences are used to correct the bad behavior, not to punish.

IRRATIONAL BELIEF and WHAT IT LEADS TO	RATIONAL BELIEF
4 It is awful and catastrophic when things are not the way I very much want them to be. **RESULT:** Leads to a lot of *frustration, anger and even rage* because life is deemed unfair and people are seen as cruel or hurtful.	It is unfortunate and disappointing when things are not the way I would like them to be, but that is not the end of the world.
5 Human unhappiness is externally caused and I have little or no ability to control my sorrows and disturbances. **RESULT:** Leads to *overwhelming sense of helplessness* where passive resignation is the rule.	Unfortunate events may happen to me that are beyond my control, but I do have control over the degree to which these negative events will upset me.
6 If something is or may be dangerous or fearsome, I should be terribly concerned about it and should keep dwelling on the possibility of its occurring. **RESULT:** Leads to *crippling anxiety* where worst-case scenarios dominate one's thinking.	If something is or may be dangerous or fearsome, I will take whatever precautions are reasonable and then forget about what I cannot control.
7 It is easier to avoid than to face certain life difficulties and self-responsibilities. **RESULT:** Leads to a life of *avoidance and irresponsibility* where there is little self-discipline to be proactive.	In the long run, it is easier to face than avoid certain life difficulties and self-responsibilities.
8 I should be dependent on others to give me support and make decisions for me. **RESULT:** Leads to a life of *childlike overdependency* where searching for others to lean on is the primary motive.	Although gathering information from experts and support from friends is quite acceptable, I am the one who makes the final decision and deals with the unpleasant situations of life.
9 My past history is an all-important determinant of my present behavior and because something once strongly affected my life, it should indefinitely have a similar effect. **RESULT:** Leads to *living perpetually in the past* where all rationales are found for passive inaction.	My past history can have an important effect on my present behavior. However, just because something once strongly affected my life, there is no reason it should continue to have a similar effect.
10 There is invariably a right, precise and perfect solution to human problems and it is catastrophic if this perfect solution is not found. **RESULT:** Leads to *inflexible perfectionism* where rigid compartmentalization is the norm. It's the refusal to accept imperfect reality.	There is seldom a right, precise and perfect solution to human problems. It is better to choose the best of the available alternatives than to search for a nonexistent perfect solution.

APPENDIX C

Medication Overview

Note: Not mentioned in the following table are medications used to treat BIPOLAR MANIA, which include the following: Lithium, Depakote, Atypical Antipsychotics (Zyprexa, Seroquel, Risperdal, Abilify, Geodon). Medications that can more generally treat BIPOLAR DISORDER include Seroquel and Lamictal. If you have been diagnosed with this disorder, discuss with your doctor which one would be best for you.

Serotonin and Norepinephrine Reuptake Inhibitors — (SNRI)

MEDICATION	DOSAGE	ADVANTAGES	DISADVANTAGES	NICHE
EFFEXOR XR (Venlafaxine) extended release capsules	37.5 mg to 375 mg	Raises serotonin and norepineph-rine. Few side effects; Very effective; Minimal sexual dysfunction; Also effective in anxiety	Initially causes nausea Can cause sweats, constipa-tion, and tremor Withdrawal/Re-bound problems; Increase BP in some people at high doses	Excellent broad spectrum; Few side effects; Can be used in combina-tion; Improves cognitive dysfunc-tion Low sexual dysfunction
CYMBALTA (Duloxetine)	30 mg to 120 mg	"Balanced" eleva-tion of serotonin and norepineph-rine; Minimal sexual dysfunction; also approved for diabetic peripheral neuropathic pain and fibromyalgia	Some nausea for the first 6 days when starting medicine	Some advantages in reducing mus-culoskeletal pain from depression and "fibromyalgia." Good for people with diabetic neu-ropathic pain. Low sexual dysfunction.
PRISTIQ	50mg, one a day for most people, 100mg once a day for some people	Cleanest of all antidepressants because it is not metabolized in the liver. Few side effects. Less rebound and BP problems with less sexual problems.	Some nausea first 6 days when start-ing the medication.	Fewer side effects than Effexor XR. Very effective and predictable in people who may be either rapid or poor metabolizers.

Selective Serotonin
Reuptake Inhibitors — (Ssri)

MEDICATION	DOSAGE	ADVANTAGES	DISADVANTAGES	NICHE
PROZAC (Fluoxetine) (Sarafem)	10 mg to 80 mg	May increase energy initially, approved for PMS syndrome, longest lasting (half life of med)	Slower onset of action; Sexual dysfunction; Long residual May cause fatigue after long-term use	Minimizes problems of noncompliance, (people forgetting to take pill) Good for PMS and anxiety, available as generic.
PAXIL (Paroxetine)	10 mg to 50 mg	Approved for depression, OCD, and panic disorder	Side effects; nausea and sedation; Sexual dysfunction	For social anxiety, OCD/panic, available as generic
ZOLOFT (Sertraline)	25 mg to 200 mg	Increases mood "middle of road" SSRI; OCD approved	Side effects; Some sedation; Sexual dysfunction	"Middle of the road SSRI" available as generic
CELEXA (Citalopram)	20 mg to 40 mg	Increase mood; Good for anxiety	Possibly less potent; Sexual dysfunction	Try when other SSRIs cause side effects or in combination, available as generic.
LEXAPRO (Escitalopram)	10 mg to 20 mg	Less side effects than CELEXA, "pure SSRI"	Some sexual dysfunction	Try when other SSRIs cause side effects or in combination
VIIBRYD (Vilazodone)	40 mg	Potent SSRI; plus raises serotonin level directly	Stomach problems with diarrhea, nausea and vomiting and insomnia	New- probably most potent in raising serotonin levels.

Other Antidepressant Medications

MEDICATION	DOSAGE	ADVANTAGES	DISADVANTAGES	NICHE
WELLBUTRIN SR WELL-BUTRIN XL APLENZIN (Bupropion)	100 mg to 300 mg 348 mg and 522 mg	Lifts mood; approved for addictions (smoking); used for ADHD; Least sexual dysfunction of all anti-depressants	May cause seizures in high doses or in people with eating disorders; Inconsistent response	Depression with fatigue, and ADHD, Addictions (smoking, overeating)
DESYREL (Trazodone)	50 mg to 400 mg	Most sedating antidepressant	Weaker at lifting mood Some morning sedation Priapism	Used in combination with other antidepressants for people with severe sleep difficulty
REMERON (Mirtazapine)	15 mg to 45 mg	Helps with insomnia Minimal sexual dysfunction	Sedation in >50% Weight gain with lower dose	Depression with insomnia; Patients with needed weight gain -(Anorexia/ wt loss)
EFFEXOR Venlafaxine immediate release tablets	37.5 mg to 375 mg	Fast acting in crisis situations	Significant side effects, particularly nausea, withdrawal rebound problems, 2 X/day dosing	Used only when a person can not afford Effexor XR. Available in generic
TRICYCLICS: Amitryptyline Doxepin Nortryptyline Imipramine others	Variable	Help with sleep Stabilize mood Help with musculoskeletal pain and headaches	Side effects including dry mouth (60%) Lethal in overdose Weight gain; Drug Interaction Orthostatic BP changes	No longer "first line" agents Good for patients with fibromyalgia and chronic pain
TRIMONOAMINE MODULATOR: Deplin	7.5mg	NO side effects	Will not work for everyone	Very safe medication to add on to an antidepressant. Also good to use in those who are taking Lamictal for Bipolar disorder.

APPENDIX D

Treatment of Depression

Depression with fatigue no anxiety	Depression with anxiety no sleep disturbance	Depression with anxiety and sleep disturbance
FIRST CHOICE Wellbutrin Pristiq Effexor XR Cymbalta	**FIRST CHOICE** Pristiq Effexor XR Cymbalta Zoloft + Wellbutrin	**FIRST CHOICE** Zoloft *(also for short-term use: add* Pristiq *Sonata, Ambien,* Lexapro *Lunesta, Rozerem)* Cymbalta Effexor XR Trazodone + 1 of the above

Psychotherapy as appropriate with all medications

Schedule for follow-up appointment in 3 weeks or call if symptoms worsen, there are increased thoughts of suicide, or side effects are intolerable.

UNSUCCESSFUL RESPONSE
Assess medication follow-through and dosage. (Side effects can be reduced by slower dose increases.) Consider adding Deplin or Abilify. Consider alternative diagnoses including Bi-polar Disorder or concomitant Attention Deficit Disorder. Switch to different medication in the same or different class (SSRI or SNRI). Consider prescribing a combination of medications. Consider psychiatric referral for evaluation.

SUCCESSFUL RESPONSE OR FULL REMISION
Goal is Hamilton Scale < 7. Monitor dosage and side effects. Office visits every 2–6 months.

APPENDIX E

Medical Conditions
Related to Depression

There are a number of general Medical conditions that can cause or, at least can be associated with depression. The following is a list of medical conditions as adapted from a compilation of medical sources.

Many, including family members and even the patients themselves, are often unaware of the fact that some of the symptoms they observe or experience in their illness are due to depression. It is not uncommon for people who suffer from a chronic illness or medical condition to also suffer from depression. But it is easily concealed by other medical problems and so, as a result, frequently goes undetected and untreated. Nonetheless, it is one of the most prevalent emotional consequences of physical illness. Typically, it reflects the stress of coping with disease; but the disease itself can also cause it.

Some studies suggest that as many as one-third of all patients with some kind of chronic medical condition also suffer from depression. This is partly due to the limitations imposed by the illness or condition on their mobility, on their ability to engage in activities they once enjoyed, and on their expectations of the future. The severity of the depression is often proportional to the severity of the illness and the limitations it imposes.

Depression can actually further complicate the medical condition (e.g., increase the risk of coronary heart disease) as well as increase the patient's fatigue and immobility. What's more, it often causes people to become isolated, further amplifying their loneliness and hopelessness. Partly because this can likewise enhance the risk of suicide, it is important to diagnose the presence of depression as early as possible.

Depression Rates Associated With Chronic Conditions

Sometimes, the combination of chronic illness and depression can make things considerably worse by giving rise to a destructive loop: The chronic condition can trigger depression which, in turn, can hamper effective treatment of the illness, which, as a consequence of continued (and perhaps, increased) pain and disability, leads to even more depression. Add to that the fact that some medications used to treat the medical condition can, themselves, cause depression, and you can have a rapidly deteriorating situation. That's why it is important to seek therapeutic help as soon as possible. It is wise, too, for friends and family to make every effort to keep the chronically ill person actively engaged with life to prevent their withdrawal—something that can otherwise likely happen.

CHRONIC CONDITION	% EXPERIENCING DEPRESSION
Heart attack	40–65%
Coronary artery disease (without heart attack)	18–20%
Parkinson's disease	40%
Multiple sclerosis	40%
Stroke	15–20%
Cancer	25% (up to 45-50% with cancer of the pancreas)
Diabetes	25%
Chronic pain syndrome	30–54%

Medications Associated With Depression

These medications are known either to have possible depressive side effects or cause depression with rapid withdrawal.*

*Adopted and modified from "Practical Pharmacology", professional seminars by Dr. Gollapudi Shankar, PharmD, MS., PH-C, BCPP, CGP.

CATEGORY	MEDICATION or TREATMENT
Blood pressure (Antihypertensives)	Reserpine (Brand name: Serpasil), Beta Blockers (e.g., Brand name: Inderal), Calcium Channel Blockers, Methyldopa (Brand name: Aldomet), Guanethidine sulfate (Brand name: Ismelin sulfate), Clonidine hydrochloride (Brand name: Catapres)
Contraceptives	Progestin-Estrogen combination (various brands), Norplant (discontinued distribution after 2002,but some still have implant)
Hormone	Estrogen (e.g., Premarin, Ogen, Estrace, Estraderm), Progesterone and derivatives (e.g., Provera, DepoProvera)
Antiparkinsons disease agents	Levodopa carbidopa (Brand name: Sinemet), Amantadine hydrochloride (Brand names: Dopar, Larodopa, Symmetrel)
Antianxiety agents-Benzodiazapines (especially withdrawal after addiction)	Diazepam (Brand name: Valium), Chlordiazepoxide (Brand name: Librium)
Psychoactive substances	Alcohol (tends to have a masking effect with depression), Opiates (e.g., Opium, Heroin, Codeine, Hydrocone, Methodone, Morphine, Oxycodone, Darvocet, Percocet, Percodan, Vicodon, to name some of the more common ones), Amphetamines, Cocaine, Anabolic steroids
Chemotherapy agents	Vincristine, vinblastine, procarbazine, Interferon.
Glucosteroids	Cortisone acetate
First Generation Antipsychotic medications	Phenothiazines (e.g., Thorazine, Mellaril, Stelazine, Trilafon, Phenergan), Haloperidol (Brand name: Haldol)

END NOTES

---

1. Stephen M. Stahl, Essential Psychopharmacology of Depression and Bipolar Disorder (Cambridge, UK: Cambridge University Press, 2000), p. 2.

2. Developed by Dr. David Kupfer, M. D.

ABOUT THE AUTHOR

Gregory M. Knopf, M.D.

Gregory M. Knopf, M.D., has been a family practice physician for 30 years and is the founder and medical director of the Gresham-Troutdale Family Medical Center. He is a graduate and Clinical Associate Professor of Family Medicine at Oregon Health Sciences University. Dr. Knopf is Board Certified in Family Medicine but has a special interest in the treatment of anxiety and depression. He speaks across the country on these topics, principally for professional audiences, and for churches and the general public as well. He has been involved in clinical research and enjoys tennis, gardening, and is active at Radiant Church in Gresham, Oregon. Dr. Knopf and his wife, Bonnie, live on a 26 acre farm and have three adult children.

Gresham-Troutdale Family Medical Center
1700 SW 257th Avenue | Troutdale, OR 97060
(503) 669-6800 Fax (503) 492-1352